You Deserve Better

Leave that abusive relationship

Mary Walsh

You Deserve Better

for Christine

Copyright ©2019 by Mary Walsh

For rights and permissions, please contact: Mary Walsh marywalshwrites@gmail.com

I left an abusive marriage.

I was lucky to get away.

I hope you are too.

The Monster is Angry

He is a monster. During your marriage, you do everything you can to keep him placated. But since you realize that you don't want to be held captive anymore, the monster is angry. You want out because you can no longer tolerate his unruly behavior. You are the only one contributing to the relationship (your time, your effort, your feelings) and it has been unbalanced for a long time. You aren't happy ever since you can remember, but he thinks, or at least tries to make you believe, everything is wonderful. You cater to him and his needs all this time and he has it made. You think if he is satisfied, then he will be nicer to you. But if anything (and I mean *anything*) doesn't go his way, he flies into a rage and blames you. Do you always give in because you don't want to cause a scene or think it's not worth it?

Does any of this sound familiar to you?

He does not respect you when he invites someone else on your vacation without talking to you first. He calls you nasty nicknames and when you ask him to stop, he says, "Can't you take a joke?" He doesn't follow anyone else's rules and thinks he is above the law. You avoid talking to him because he doesn't acknowledge you or turns every serious conversation into a fight. You are tired of fighting. All. The. Time. You wonder if he hates himself so much that he must constantly put you down to make himself feel better. But no one is entitled to be an asshole. Even if his mother died when he was a teenager, that doesn't give him the right to be a dick.

In your marriage, he loves the situation; he does not love you. You are a piece of property to him. He treats you like he hates you. He doesn't care about your issues. He doesn't respond to your emails or texts because he can't be bothered. Stop making excuses for him. Stop rewarding his bad behavior. He is a mean and vicious person. Things will not get better. He does not care if he makes you cry. Better yet, he *wants* you to cry. It makes him feel like a man.

Here is a non-comprehensive list of abusive traits my ex-husband had. If you recognize some or all of these in your partner, your situation will not get better.

- He doesn't apologize. Ever.
- He has no remorse or empathy.
- He refuses to spend time with you but gives you a tough time if you do something without him.
- He kisses the dog goodnight and not you.

- He has zero respect for women or anyone who isn't exactly like him - a heterosexual man - because he believes he is better than everyone else.
- He makes fun of anyone who is different from him – if they have pink hair or multiple facial piercings.
- He believes he is more important than you.
- He doesn't take responsibility for his actions and turns on people if they don't agree with him.
- He threatens not to do something with you or throws your dinner in the trash if things don't go how HE wants them.
- He refuses to go to your work events or your friends' weddings saying he doesn't have to do anything except pay taxes and die.
- He complains about *everything*.
- He says that you nag him but only because he doesn't answer you the first two times you say something to him.

Would you cry at his funeral?

Would you feel relieved that he is out of your life for good?

This is the most important part. If he threatens to leave you because he thinks you are "acting up", **let him**. If he says, "Well if you don't like it, you can leave", **then do it**. Take pleasure in moving out because he refuses to. If you have reached your breaking point, it's time to leave. If he is offended when you tell him you deserve better, don't feel sorry for him. If he believes he is treating you well because he is not a drunk and doesn't hit you, thank him for setting the bar so low and walk out the door.

The definition of insanity is doing the same thing over and over again and expecting different results. He won't change. *You* must change. A nice, normal person won't crucify you for a simple mistake or a minor disagreement. He is not normal.

When you leave, you will upset his utopia and he will want it back. He will do everything he can to hurt you. He will try to keep the kids from you. He doesn't care about them nor does he want them. He only knows if he keeps them from you, he will hurt you. He will blame you if you don't let them be with him. If he tries to prevent you from talking to them on the phone, get them their own phone. He *wants* to hurt you again and again. He knows how to push your buttons. Simply tell him "Thank you for reminding me why I left you." He will try to play on your kindness. He has pushed you to the point where you no longer give a fuck about him.

Even though a divorce will be horrific, embrace it. He will rage at you even more than he ever has. He will try to convince you that this is a "silly momentary lapse" of your judgment and assumes that you will be coming back to him. He does not want you to think that he believes you are serious. He will pressure you to come back. (Don't do it!) He will guilt you for breaking up the family. He will try to tempt you with gifts. He will try to turn the kids against you and tell them lies about you. He will make empty promises that he will be a better person. Remind yourself that it's too little, too late. No matter what he says, he knows deep down that you are right, and he's scared to death. As long as he is running scared, you will win.

He will try to make you "pay" for leaving him. He will try to destroy you. He won't play fair. He refused to go to marriage counseling for years but insists that you need to go now that you have had enough (sorry to say this but you may have to go - check your state law minimum requirements). He will cut off his nose to spite his face, so he can win against you (he will stop paying the mortgage to hurt you but will hurt his credit in the process). Expect that he will drag the divorce out as long as possible until a judge forces him to sign the paperwork.

You cannot think that he will ever be rational or cooperative. Don't ever worry that anyone will judge you why you left him. They will finally ask you if you are okay because they didn't want to get involved earlier. But they saw and heard everything. People noticed.

But you will win. To win is to get out of the divorce alive. Always keep your eye on the target: freedom from abuse.

If you make more money than him, be prepared for him to file for child support and spousal support against you. Yes, it sucks, but he could be entitled to it.

He may stalk you and drive by your house because he can't stand that you are happy and functioning without him. If he badgers you because he wants to see you or insists on knowing what you're doing, tell him that you "have plans." Immediately call or go to the police if you ever feel threatened or scared. Do everything you can to protect yourself. The abusive personality knows no bounds.

* * *

"There will be a time when loud-mouthed, incompetent people seem to be getting the best of you. When that happens, you only have to be patient and wait for them to self-destruct. It never fails." – Richard Rybolt

His Behavior is Not Normal

Below are real-life personality examples from my abusive marriage. Read them and be honest with yourself. How many of them fit your situation? Every partner can be an idiot from time to time, but if these or similar situations define your life, you need to take action. Immediately. Only you know what that action should be, whether it's seeking personal or marital counseling, talking to a friend or relative, or planning your exit strategy. Take action now.

Does he purposely do things to make you angry or annoyed? You ask him to clean the counter after he makes toast and he wipes the crumbs right on the floor right in front of you.

Does he refuse to do anything special for you for Mother's Day saying, "Why? You're not MY mother"? And refuse to take the kids so that you get a break?

Does he refuse to help you but insist that you help him? He won't stop eating his ice cream as you are lugging groceries in the house but demands that you help him shovel the snow.

Does he scream at you that you aren't watching where you are going if you bump into him, but also screams at you because you are in his way when he bumps into you?

Does he expect you to do everything around the house? He refuses to help you do the kids' laundry, clean up after dinner, make the kids' lunches, walk the dogs, take the garbage out, vacuum, empty the dishwasher, remount the towel rack after *he* knocked it down...

Does he always put his family (or the dog) before you saying blood is thicker than water? And refuse to spend time with your family or think that you shouldn't spend money on your family at Christmas?

Does he tell you he'll be home in 10 minutes then not show up for two hours and tell you it's none of your business where he's been?

Does he refuse to tell you his upcoming events to put into the family calendar and tell you not to worry about what *he* is doing?

Does he balk at or flat out refuse any idea you have saying "Why would I want to do that?"

Does he blame you for his bad behavior? When you tell him not to be a jerk to someone, he says "Well you married me."

Does he expect everyone to cater to him and to do what HE wants, thinks, and feels?

Does he refuse to hold your hand in public?

Does he fly into a rage or have a temper tantrum when things don't go his way?

Does he have to be right about everything even when he is clearly wrong – when he screams at you insisting that Texas is the largest state?

Does he question the money you spend when you spend $130 on groceries for the family but thinks it's okay for him to drop $1000 on a new basketball hoop?

Does he make fun of the things you like and talk bad about your friends?

Does he have to win at <u>everything</u>? Even his sister-in-law's baby shower games...

Does he have to have the last word?

Does he make you feel like nothing you say or do is good enough? Does he treat you like he has complete control over everything and that you don't get a vote?

Does he dictate what he thinks you should wear, where you go, or who you spend time with? Then give you a hard time if you refuse what he wants you to do or make you feel guilty or unimportant?

Does he constantly put you down?

Does he take the TV remote and change the channel in the middle of a show that you are watching?

Does he say, "Everyone is entitled to one mistake... and mine was our wedding day?"

Does he act like he is perfect and never makes any mistakes? Does he expect you to be perfect and scream at you when you aren't?

Does he delete your phone messages before you have a chance to hear them?

Does he have total disregard for your career? Does he think that you should be the maid and the nanny of the house, in addition to working your income-earning job, and acts like he doesn't have to lift a finger?

Does he say he doesn't have time to answer your texts, but you can clearly see that he has answered texts from other people?

Does he not care about your feelings and gets off seeing you cry?

Does he scream at you until he verbally beats you to a pulp? Leaving you feeling beaten, wounded, battered, bruised, and torn?

More than a Narcissist

Plenty of articles exist online with the headline "Did you marry a narcissist?" and list all the characteristics of one. A narcissist is "someone who is overly self-involved, and often vain and selfish."

Simple narcissists have huge egos, experiencing intense vanity and selfishness, and need constant admiration. Sociopaths are similar, having an inflated sense of self and entitlement. They tend to blame others for their failures. They also break the law or social rules because they think they are above those rules.

He is a sociopath. Sociopaths' disregard for others begins in childhood or early adolescence and continues into adulthood. They don't think the rules apply to them and will put other people in harm's way to benefit themselves. On top of that, they don't feel bad about it — they have no remorse. You'll find that a lot of people simply don't like them.

A sociopath is disrespectful, insensitive, controlling, bullying, uses threats and intimidation, lies, disregards your feelings, minimizes and trivializes, gives you the silent treatment, rages, throws tantrums, is never accountable, is a hypocrite, projects on you, does not show sympathy or remorse, exploits, is arrogant and condescending, acts superior, uses demands, commands, and orders, does not listen, is a know it all, and can have a charming exterior personality until he is enraged or things don't go his way. It boils down to an overgrown, weak, fearful, immature bully, needing control, with a sense of entitlement and a false sense of power.

Sure, anyone might find themselves married to someone who seems to constantly think only about themselves. Let's face it. Aren't we all that way occasionally? We are human. But, this is different. He is vicious and abusive. He threatens to hit you but doesn't, but you still feel like you've been punched in the face too many times. Do you want to stick around to see if he really will?

No one goes into a marriage thinking they will get a divorce. But does he throw his ring at you three months after the wedding saying it has been the worst time of his life? Or does he threaten to have you arrested for taking his car? He might not methodically outright plan to see how you react, but he sees he can get away with things like that. Even if you *tell* him that what he did was awful, he sees that you are still there and haven't left yet. He will continue to do it... until you leave.

You ask yourself, "why didn't I leave the first time?" Because you didn't want to fail or easily give up. You lost count of how many times he treated you like that...because it wasn't an isolated incident. I don't know if there are any surveys on this topic, but I would bet that most marriages that end in divorce should have ended during the first six months but for one partner's desire not to fail.

Maybe you fell for his charm in the beginning because he made you feel good. Sociopaths can be disarmingly charming when they want to be. Maybe you felt bad for him that his mother died at such an early age. Maybe he reminded you (consciously or subconsciously) of your parent who treated you the same way.

While you contemplate your future, you are inundated with questions and that's normal.

- Why are you even with this guy?
- Maybe love happened at one point but are you merely existing in the relationship now?
- Are you scared of change?
- Do you even like him anymore?
- Are you afraid you'll get nothing if you divorce?

If you are there because of the kids, they will be okay.

- Are you afraid that your kids will be mad at you for disrupting their lives?
- Do you think he'll get better if you sacrifice your self-worth and dignity?
- Do you not want to give up the BMW or the 4000 square foot home?
- Are you afraid of being alone?
- Do you think you need a reason to leave?
- Do you make excuses for his unruly behavior?
- Do you think you failed at marriage if you leave?
- Were you young and naïve to good, nurturing relationships?
- Do you think he'll treat you even worse if you leave?
- Do you even remember why you two got together in the first place? (Did you chase him?)

None of these are a good reason to stay with a man who constantly treats you like garbage.

If he's not doing anything to keep you, why are you fighting so hard to stay?

Enough is Enough

I won't lie to you. This will suck. Big time. Leaving him will be one of the hardest and most brutal times of your life. But you <u>will</u> get through it. I won't sugarcoat anything. Your body will feel like your skin is falling off your bones every time you take a step. You won't sleep much. You won't want to eat. You'll probably lose weight. You'll likely go to the doctor and she might run all sorts of tests thinking you have an ulcer, but you tell her you are under a lot of stress. A lot. Yeah, this will suck. You will cry - and probably scream a little. You'll scream at him so much that your neighbors might call you saying you're being too loud. You will feel exhausted and drained. You will have a lot of bad days. But each day will be better than the last. It is not your fault that he is an awful, awful man. You will disrupt your kids' lives. They will be mad at you for a while. They will blame you for breaking up the family. But do you want your son to think that it's okay to treat people the way you are treated? Do you want your daughter to think that it's okay to *be* treated like this?

But if you are reading this, you already know that you've been to the bottom of hell. Now the only place to go is up.

You'll encounter many traps and herculean obstacles along the way. You might want to give up because it will be hard, but you will eventually get to the top. And when you get to the top, you'll be free. Freer than you've ever felt. Free like a new puppy who broke out of her cage. Free like a little kid running the empty streets at Disney World. Free like you have never felt before. In the end, after you've climbed to the top with bumps and bruises and scars along the way, you'll feel the best you've ever felt.

Because... my sister, you won't ever have anyone question you for that extra $10 you want to spend on a t-shirt or be berated in public for voicing that he left you alone for an hour without telling you where he was going, or do everything that HE wants to do, or have someone blame you for their bad behavior, or make you feel like you aren't worth anything.

But you are.

You are worth someone being nice to you. You are worth someone asking how your day was without interrupting you to call someone else while you are talking.

You are good enough.

You are worth someone helping you around the house. You are worth someone being your arm candy without complaining or making fun of everyone at your event. You are worth someone having your back when you discipline the kids.

You have the power to end the vicious cycle. You are a strong, wonderful, lovable person who deserves better.

You are worth it.

Have a Plan

Now that you know that you deserve better, you'll want to get away from him as fast as possible. Don't do it. Now you're probably thinking "Wait... what did you say? *Don't* get away from him?" Yes, get away from him, but don't blindly leave him without a plan. Don't pack up your things one night and take the kids. He will hunt you down and practically tear those kids right out of your arms. You need to take the time to be ready to leave him. It might take you a month. It might take you a year. But have a plan. And remember, always stay safe. If you believe you need protection, include that in your plan. Don't leave it to chance.

Keep a journal and write everything down. I mean everything. If he balks at you when you ask him to take out the trash, write it down. If he publicly berates and humiliates you because you are telling a kid not to climb high in a tree because you're afraid he'll fall, write it down. If he screams at you about giving your friend $40 as a wedding present because you didn't consult with him first, write it down.

Make copies of everything pertaining to your marriage and children. Make copies of everyone's birth certificates, social security cards, passports, mortgage information, last pay stubs, tax information, credit card information, utilities, savings bonds, car information, debt, wills. Everything. Get a portable fireproof safe because that's easier to carry and take what you can with you.

Have a trusted friend keep getaway cash. Depending on where you live, you'll need at least $1000 in cash when you leave. He cannot trace cash so keep it in a safe place. You'll need the money to put down a deposit on an apartment and pay for rent, food, and anything else you might need. If you are not working, you'll probably need a few thousand in cash. You may also need a cosigner if you are leasing an apartment in your name and have no verifiable income. You'll eventually get alimony and child support, but the cash will be a nice buffer until that money comes. If you have the option of divorcing in a state where child support is paid until age 21, do it. New York, for example, is one of those states.

Find a bulldog attorney. You will need someone who will fight for you and not wait for something to happen. Overdress when you go to court and always cooperate with the judge. Unless you had a prenup, you are probably entitled to half of everything. Check the divorce laws in your state. Some states grant you a divorce in as little as 90 days. Others say you need to be separated for at least a year or two. Be prepared that he will fight you every step of the way and will drag it out as long as possible.

Separate all joint assets and debts as soon as possible. Open your own bank account. Close all joint credit card accounts. If he refuses to pay a joint debt like a mortgage or a car payment, you are still responsible for the whole thing. You might love your big house, but if you cannot afford it on your own, you will need to sell it. If he refuses to help list it, your bulldog attorney can file a motion to force him to do it.

Find a safe place to live. You might have to live with family for a while or rent a minuscule apartment with a neighbor who blares the TV at 3 a.m. or wayward chickens run across the street in front of you. But if the place has a deadbolt on it, you can always ask your neighbor to turn down his TV and you'll have to wait until the chickens cross the road.

Get a custody agreement in place as fast as possible. He WILL try to keep the kids from you if you don't have an agreement set up. He will even try to keep the kids from you on Mother's Day. File for full custody if he repeatedly leaves the kids with someone else on his time. Use the reality that courts generally favor children being in the physical custody of the mother to your advantage.

Gradually pack up everything you want to keep safe. He will notice if you take a bed or dresser, but you can slowly pack up the kids' scrapbooks and mementos that you are afraid he'll destroy if he finds out you are leaving him. Leave on a night when you know he won't be there because he <u>will</u> try to stop you. He may even physically block the door so that you can't leave. Pack everything into your car and go. Don't look back. You are doing the right thing.

Be prepared to fight. Get out your armor. Sharpen your sword. Polish your shield. Know that he will fight you every step of the way. He will stiff you if he owes you money. He will try to keep the kids from you. He will try to keep your belongings from you until a judge orders him to give them to you. He will call you names and try to intimidate you. He may even beg you to come back promising he will be better. *Expect* that he won't cooperate. You will win.

DOs and DON'Ts
– after you leave him

DO NOT bash him on Facebook. Even though he has no heart and is doing everything in his power to hurt you, do not put anything in writing that might come back to haunt you. You can scream and curse at him all you want in person, but do not put anything malicious in a text, on a voice message, or social media. He WILL use it against you. (Except for Virginia, it is illegal in most states to record conversations without the other person's knowledge.) You'll get nothing from trying to hurt him. You'll be tempted to reply to his nasty text because he is fishing for a reaction out of you, but <u>always</u> take the high road and be the bigger person. Stooping to his level will always come back to bite you.

DO take a trip by yourself. If it's simply a road trip for the day to antique shops or a week-long vacation to Greece, do something for yourself and by yourself. You love your kids and want to do things with them, but this trip is for you. You don't have to worry about anyone ruining your vacation because he refused to help you carry a heavy backpack around Disney World. Nor do you have to worry about your kids running in five different directions. This trip is for you to relax, go at your own pace, and do what you want without anyone rushing you. You can take your kids next time.

DO understand Wants vs. Needs. Yes, you need food in your fridge and the kids need clothes to wear, but do you really need $100 Vera Wang heels? Save that money. You never know when your car will need a new set of tires or when the water heater will need to be replaced. You are now the sole person who oversees the financial needs of your household. Spend wisely and save wisely. Make a point of saving ten percent of your income, no matter how low it is at this point.

DO paint your kitchen. Paint your kitchen yellow. Bright colors are an instant mood lifter and remind you every day that you have made the right decision to be on your own. Not only that, painting is a therapeutic and tangible sense of accomplishment. (If you rent, be sure to get approval from your property owner first.)

DO get everything in writing. If he has promised to split the kids' soccer registration fees, get it in writing. If he says that he will return the kids to you at a certain time, get it in writing. Do not trust him on his word. He will lie, cheat, and steal from you to hurt you. Keep every email and text he sends you. Take everything you have in writing to your bulldog attorney and use the courts to assist in getting these things in writing.

DO be patient. The divorce may take years (yes, I said YEARS!) to finalize. Remember that every day you are on your own in your tiny apartment is better than any day with him in a monster house.

DO NOT trash talk him to your kids. They already know there is tension in the family. They aren't dumb. As much as you want to, don't call him a douchebag in front of your kids. This will always come back to bite you. He is their father and they may defend him no matter what he does. Besides, it makes you look weak. You can, however, talk to your kids about their father's poor behavior and that it's never nice to treat people the way he does. They will eventually learn that their father is a douchebag. Your college-age son will come to you first when he wants a tattoo because he knows you won't judge him. Your teenage daughter will seek you out for a compassionate shoulder.

DO be fair and cordial to him. He doesn't deserve your kindness but show respect even to people who don't deserve it; not as a reflection of their character but as a reflection of yours. Your kids will learn from you.

DO try something new. Take a cooking class. Learn to salsa dance. Do something you always wanted to do but couldn't because he either made fun of you for it or made you feel guilty about leaving him even though he wanted nothing to do with you.

DO make yourself laugh at his expense. No, don't pay for a billboard bashing him. Do something simple as finding an awful ringtone for him - like a frog who has swallowed a bag of rocks, so it makes you laugh every time you hear it. Plus, when you hear it, you know not to pick it up if you don't want to talk to him.

DO NOT answer his every call. He might think you are still at his beck and call, but you are not. And if he calls and doesn't leave a message, do not call him back. If he can't be bothered to leave a message, then it must not be important. And do not take his call after 10 p.m. That's rude of him and he does not respect your boundaries.

DO change your name back. Take the steps to go back to your maiden name. It's yours and you were born with it.

Going back to your maiden name is one thing he can do nothing about. Besides, do you want someone coming up to you at a future time asking you if you are related to him?

DO lean on your friends. Know that some will take his side. That's okay. You'll be fine without them. Make new ones – at your cooking class.

DO treat him the same way he treats you. If he refuses to give you the kids' passports until the morning of your trip, do the same thing to him for his trip. It's not who you are but do it anyway – in a cordial and objective way, of course. He won't like it, but you already know that.

DO NOT go on a date with someone new for at least six months. You need to get your shit together first. You will go through myriad emotions and you need to deal with them on your own. You want to be your best for someone new. Wait.

DO remember you are tougher than you think you are. You are strong and awesome! You will get through this. You might question if you are doing the right thing. You are. If you give up, he wins. Do not second guess yourself.

DO know that this uncertainty is only temporary. Recovery takes time. You will like who you become. You are beautiful and kind and good. You don't find your worth in a man. You find your worth within yourself. Then find a man who is worthy of you. Remember that.

Moving On

Know that you will have flashbacks, possibly mild PTSD, and bouts of depression. You'll feel sad, tired, invigorated, and happy. Let these feelings happen but go see a shrink to help yourself.

You'll listen more carefully when you hear about another woman being treated like crap and you'll want to help her escape the same prison that you were in.

You will be hesitant when someone treats you with kindness, wants nothing in return, and is interested in you. They ask you how your day is and genuinely listen. You will believe that you will meet good people. They do exist.

He is replaceable. But don't make that your immediate goal.

Don't worry about breaking his heart because he has no heart to break. If, in the unlikely scenario that he grows one, the people in his life will have you to thank.

If you ever feel he is hurting or mentally abusing your kids, immediately go to Child Services. He no longer has you to verbally beat up, so he may take it out on them.

He is not your responsibility anymore. Do not help him out. Learn to say no. You owe him nothing.

Remember that you are free from him. You can hang up on him or walk away.

Every ounce of hate for him will surface from deep inside your body. You've been suppressing it for years until now. You may not forgive him for a long time – or ever. But don't let the anger eat you up. You have moved on from that incarceration.

You never have to be treated like that again. You can have a good, happy life. You are responsible for your happiness now.

Remember that stuff can be replaced. It's just stuff. You can always get a new phone number, a new couch, a new car...

Cut yourself some slack. You can't do everything. Do what you can and move on. You'll probably argue with your kids about wearing a jacket when it's 20 degrees out but remember that you are happy. Little bumps may happen along the way but, in the end, all is good. Keep moving forward.

Teach your kids kindness every day.

The holidays will probably be hard for you. You might feel alone but it's better than spending another holiday on edge with him. It's okay to miss the family unit even though you don't miss him.

You might not be with your kids 24/7 anymore. They know you still love them and would do anything for them. A mother's love never ceases. Take advantage of your alone time to develop the new you.

His family and friends will probably take his side regardless of how he behaves. You will be the bad guy in their eyes for leaving him. Know that their opinion no longer matters.

The Horizon is in Sight

Going through a divorce and being a single mom for 10 years was one of the toughest things I've ever had to do. I had hit my breaking point and was tired of being treated like crap. Some days I wanted to curl up in a ball and stay in bed. My body took a toll and I lost a bunch of weight. I felt like a failure. I constantly doubted myself and wondered if I was on the right path. Some days I didn't want to see anyone and other times I insisted on being surrounded by friends. Nights alone were hard. But I couldn't go back to the way things were. Not if I wanted a better life for myself.

I had two young children who relied on me. They were six and nine when I left their dad. I pushed through days with sheer will. Being their mom forced me. If I didn't do it, who would? I couldn't disappoint my kids. That was not an option. They had gone through enough by losing their family unit. I couldn't let them down again.

Per the custody arrangement, my kids were with me every other full week. It was tough on me to go a week without them, but our week together gave them a place to hang their hat for a while. Some divorced parents I knew swapped their kids every other day. I couldn't do that to my kids. They needed stability even though I missed them when they weren't with me.

I set up a routine and normalcy for them. Bedtime was at 9:00 (later as they got older). They had to fold their laundry on Sundays and pack their school lunches. No phones were allowed at the dinner table. Homework had to be done on time and before playtime. When we went out to eat, I made them order for themselves to boost their self-confidence and make decisions for themselves in public.

My custody weeks were dedicated to my kids. We'd play at the park, go to movies, and walk to the nearby ice cream shop. We'd bake cookies together and build forts with the couch cushions. I always tried to say "Yes" to them. Trips to the grocery store and my appointments could wait for my off-weeks.

I hated Sundays when they returned to their dad. Deep down, I think they did too, but I couldn't project my wants onto them. They needed to be with him, even though he tried to keep them from me on Mother's Day a few times. When he refused to let me talk to them on the phone for no other reason than he was being a jerk, I got my kids cheap cell phones.

When my kids were with their dad, my home was empty. Clean, but empty. Shoes left all over the floor more than made up for being alone. I was forced to spend every other holiday on my own and sometimes I could barely hold it together. Even though Day 100 of being a single mom didn't feel much different from Day 99, it was leaps and bounds better than Day 1. I didn't know it then, but I was on my way to establishing a good life for my kids.

I had these simple house rules for my kids and the rest fell into place:

- Don't lie
- Be respectful
- Do your chores
- Be home on time
- Clean up after yourself

If my kids broke a rule, consequences occurred. I followed through on punishments without hesitation. Being outnumbered, I had to teach my kids that I was in charge or they would have walked all over me. Once, when my daughter and her elementary-school friend climbed out on our porch roof, she was grounded for a week. If my son left trash on the kitchen counter and went to bed, I left it there until the next morning and made him throw it away.

Did my kids get mad at me sometimes? Absolutely. But what child *doesn't* disagree with their mother? It's a rite of passage growing up. My kids weren't especially thrilled with me when I made them go to church either. ("Ugh, Mom, do we *have* to??")

Despite my best efforts, I tried so hard not to talk badly about their dad. Sometimes I failed. They even caught me a few times screaming at him on the phone. My hate for him overwhelmed me and I had a tough time fighting it off all the time. When that happened, I stressed to my kids that his <u>behavior</u> was unacceptable, not him. I had to keep the high road for their sake.

After two-and-a-half years of renting, I bought a house and things were looking up for the three of us. My kids were thrilled about having a yard of their own and two full bathrooms. A year later, we adopted a dog. I had an 'open door' policy at the house and my kids' friends were always welcome no matter what I had planned. Two more for dinner? No problem! (A few years later, my daughter's friend found a safe haven at my house because she was being physically abused by her mother.)

Owning a home with one income, I watched my spending like a hawk. Even though I had a good-paying job, I clipped coupons, looked for sales, and scoured second-hand shops. I never knew if my water heater would break so I saved money where I could. Falling into debt was not an option and, as a result, my credit score flourished. A few times, my checkbook balance dipped below $100, but I never bounced a check. If getting a new pair of shoes didn't fit into my budget, I went without. I made sure I had food in our fridge and clothes in my kids' closets. They might not have had UGG boots or Vineyard Vines pullovers, but they had everything they needed.

When my kids were in elementary school, I often volunteered in their classrooms and at their school functions. They needed to know that their mom was there for them and supported them. I was always at their sporting events, too. Many weekends were spent at soccer and baseball fields. If someone asked me out to dinner on my weeks with my kids, I declined. My kids came first. Always.

I raised them alone. I had no choice but to do everything myself. My family was states away. Friends helped occasionally but they had their own kids to take care of. Pride prevented me from relying on anyone else. I had to do it and I did my best. If I failed as a mother, I had no one to blame but myself. My kids' fate was in my hands.

Did I stumble sometimes? Absolutely. My son made fun of me for burning bacon all the time. On a few occasions, I forgot to send in school permission slips. (Yikes.) More often than not, I was there for my kids and they knew it. I just asked that they gave me more than 12 hours' notice to put together a history project!

I couldn't tell my kids the details of why I left their dad. They had to figure it out for themselves and I refused to create a division between them and their father. Once they reached high school, they were enlightened by his bad behavior. I just had to remain patient (as hard as it was) and it worked out in my favor when they turned to me.

My kids and I had an appetite for wanderlust. We'd take day trips to Baltimore, Philadelphia, and Washington, DC. If I pushed anything on them over the course of their lives, it was the gift of travel. In 2017, I had saved enough money to take my kids on a trip to Europe. The three of us spent a week in Venice, Rome, and Paris. Did we stay in 5-star hotels and dine at luxury restaurants? Not even close. But we rode a gondola in the Grand Canal, toured The Vatican, and climbed the steps of the Eiffel Tower because I could afford it. The trip was something they'd never forget.

The first time I realized that I did right by my kids was in 2018 when my son got his first tattoo. He was 18 ½ and was legally allowed to get one on his own, but he chose to tell me about it beforehand. My proud smile stretched from ear to ear. He hadn't told his dad and didn't have plans to do so. Despite my selfish inner objections, I convinced him to tell his dad so that he didn't get screamed at afterward. I looked out for my son even though I didn't have to. I hoped he appreciated that.

Ever since then, my kids have come to me about jobs, sex, smoking, cooking, and budgeting their money. It warms my heart to know that we have a respectful dynamic and they can talk openly with me. I treat them like the young adults that they are and they trust me with most of their inner secrets. But I'm realistic that my kids won't tell me everything. When my son was in college, I found pot in his room. What was I gonna do? Ground him? He was an adult and could make decisions for himself - even though I didn't agree with it.

My kids are in their early 20s now. My son is in med school and my daughter is studying neuroscience in undergrad. They both have been blessed to travel to China, England, Spain, and Costa Rica through school. Not only have they excelled in the classroom, but they've succeeded in *life*.

When they were seniors in high school, my son was a starter on his soccer and basketball teams and my daughter was captain of her field hockey team. Nowadays, my son posts pics of his cooking prowess on Instagram (ratatouille anyone?) and my daughter volunteers with Big Brothers Big Sisters. They are kind, confident, and well-rounded. They aren't afraid to initiate conversations and strive to do the right thing. Many of my kids' teachers, coaches, and friends' parents have told me that they were a joy to know.

This Mama Bear is so proud of both of them.

I'm a survivor of domestic abuse. But don't pity me. One step (and year) at a time, I had rebuilt my life as a single parent. When someone tells me that I have good kids, that's all the validation I need to know that I made the right decision to leave. My horizon is reached.

Final Thoughts

You are important.

Your wants matter.

In failure, we often garner our most strength and wisdom.

Divorce does not define you. New beginnings are coming your way.

You might not have your life planned out... and that's okay.

Be Strong when you are weak.
Be Brave when you are scared.
Be Humble when you are victorious.
Be Badass every day!
- Michelle Moschetti

Additional Assistance

Contact The National Domestic Violence Hotline – www.thehotline.org

Safety Alert from www.thehotline.org: Computer use can be monitored and is impossible to completely clear. If you are afraid your internet usage might be monitored, call the National Domestic Violence Hotline at 1-800-799-7233 or TTY 1-800-787-3224.

Please share this book with anyone who you think might need it.

*Songs for you**

Hurt - Chase Goehring

Treat you better – Shawn Mendes

Over you – Daughtry

Since U been gone – Kelly Clarkson

Too little, too late – JoJo

All I have – Jennifer Lopez

The heart of the matter – Don Henley

Love remains the same – Gavin Rossdale

Ordinary people – John Legend

Cry me a river – Justin Timberlake

If you're gone – Matchbox 20

Better man – Pearl Jam

There you go – P!nk

Sober – P!nk

Dead & gone – TI

Apologize – Timberland

Irreplaceable – Beyoncé

So what – P!nk

Piece by piece – Kelly Clarkson

Rise up – Andra Day

Survivor – Destiny's Child

If I were a boy – Beyoncé

I saw the sign – Ace of Base

You're not the only one – Joseph Gordon-Levitt

*None of these artists are affiliated with this book. These songs are my personal choices.

Thank you for reading my book.
If you enjoyed it, won't you please take a moment to leave
me a review at your favorite retailer?
One or two sentences are perfectly fine.
Help an author out. ☺
Thanks!

Want some cool merch from me?
Post a pic of this book on your social media and tag me!
@marywalshwrites

Tag me on:

**Sign up for my sometimes-monthly newsletter and
order autographed books at:**

marywalshwrites.com

Follow me on Goodreads and Amazon:

www.goodreads.com/goodreadscommarywalshwrites
www.amazon.com/author/marywalsh2

Other titles by Mary Walsh

The Curse of Jean Lafitte
Knights of the Corporate Round Table
American Posse
Memories of 9/11
Plenty of Fish in the Ocean State
Once Upon a Time in Chicago
Fine Spirits Served Here
Dragon Slayer
Stable of Studs
Catch a Break
Life Lessons for My Kids
Where or When
His Second Chance
Wounded but not Dead